THE TWELVE RAYS

PRACTICAL APPLICATIONS

Foundational Level Individual Workbook

Michael G. Love

SPARK Publications
Charlotte, North Carolina

The Twelve Rays Practical Applications:
Foundational Level Individual Workbook
Michael G. Love

Designed, produced, and published by SPARK Publications
SPARKpublications.com
Charlotte, North Carolina

Printed in the United States of America.
First Edition, May 2019, ISBN: 978-1-943070-61-9

CONTENTS

Fetter not thy Soul in bondage of darkness; free, let it wing in its flight to the stars.

- THE EMERALD TABLETS OF
THOTH THE ATLANTEAN

INTRODUCTION

You are about to embark on a personal journey through the first three Rays. This first workshop, the Foundational Workshop, is designed to help you embrace the Divine within yourself. Think of these Rays as our Divine Inheritance. It is, however, an inheritance that most have never heard of. While these introductory examples, that you will learn today, demonstrate the efficacy of the Rays, the real challenge before us all is to embrace our Divine Heritage.

Our Western society has been schooled in many different philosophies and religious ideologies. Some of them empower us, while others disempower us. Some invite us to challenge the status quo, while others admonish us to defend it.

The first three Rays' attributes that I describe in this workbook are ours to own. Use them freely and frequently, and as you do, you will use your creativity to find different ways to apply your Divine talents. I think the biggest challenge for all of us is to take this understanding of who we are and what we are capable of being and to live it every day.

In this workshop, you will learn five specific techniques that use the first three Rays and are of everyday, practical value. We will begin with resistance to change. This is the same as feeling stuck. Then we will use the same approach to help you to reduce stress in your everyday life. The third technique focuses on reducing the feelings of loneliness. Then we will learn two techniques to use the Third Ray to manifest our desires. One of these techniques has been used with the Law of Attraction for decades.

The second workshop in this series focuses on Rays Four through Seven. This is the Life Experiences Workshop. In this workshop, you will learn techniques that use the Rays of Attributes, also called the Rays of Experience. The Team (more on them later) said, "It is these energies that the individual can use in your experience, in your life experience to raise yourself through the hardships you create, through the trials, through the challenges." The Seventh Ray is of particular interest because many of you may have heard of it already. The Seventh Ray is also called the Violet Flame of St. Germain.

The third workshop in this series is the Soul Integration Workshop. In this workshop, you will work with the new Rays, Rays Eight through Twelve, which we refer to as the Rays of Soul Integration. You will be introduced to techniques that help you to establish contact with your soul-level consciousness using the Ninth Ray. Then you will learn about the Body of Light, the Tenth Ray, and actually have the opportunity to begin to anchor the Body of Light into your current physical body here in this dimension. Beyond the Tenth Ray is the Bridge to the New Awareness and then the Twelfth Ray itself, which is referred to as the New Awareness.

These new Rays represents an expansion of your soul-level consciousness into this dimension. Humankind has now reached a point where this level of advancement is being offered to us. Let me just point out that reaching this point individually takes a fair amount of focused intention to raise your personal energetic level through the techniques presented in these workshops using the Rays.

Let's turn our attention now back to this Foundational Workshop. Allow me to suggest that you are going to need three things to get the most out of this workshop. The first thing that you want to have with you are personal goals. If you are here because you are curious, that is fine, but curiosity will only get you so far. If you are here to find answers to questions that are important to you, that will take you further. If you are here to achieve a specific personal goal, for example to heal yourself, that is better. This workshop is about getting answers and moving forward.

The second thing you will need is motivation. Curiosity is a type of motivation, but as I mentioned earlier, it will only take you so far. Do you have motivation beyond curiosity? You will need plenty of motivation when it comes time to move forward. Many individuals know what is causing them to feel stuck, but few have the motivation to move forward. You may feel stuck in a job, or a relationship, or a physical condition like smoking or being overweight, or just feeling like nothing you ever attempt succeeds. With the proper motivation, you can move beyond any of those conditions.

The third thing that you need is a set of tools. This is where I can help. The Twelve Rays are your personal tools to help you create the life that you desire here in this physical dimension. Obviously, there are other ways to achieve your goals. The Twelve Rays give you the ability to more efficiently achieve the goals you set for yourself. In this workshop, we are going to focus on the first three Rays.

These Rays are all about personal power. Now, I know that term gets used a lot these days. This personal empowerment that I am referring to comes from embracing your personal divinity. The divinity that is in you and me and everyone on this planet. If you have ever taken a yoga class, you have probably heard the Sanskrit greeting *namasté*. One of the most common translations of *namasté* is "the divine light in me bows to the divine light within you."

This may be a new idea for you. Or perhaps it is an idea that you have contemplated in the past but weren't quite ready to embrace. Then again, you may be in perfect agreement with it. If you are still undecided about the notion of your divinity, I ask you to not let that stop you from experiencing the Rays. Keep an open mind and see if you feel any different after this workshop.

There are different ways to conceptualize our personal divinity. The conceptualization that we will be discussing today is embodied in the Twelve Rays. They are, in my opinion, a modern metaphor for what has been described in hundreds, perhaps thousands of different cultures for thousands of years—our longing to know who we are and how we came to be here.

The Twelve Rays metaphor contains a modern version of the creation story well suited for our digital age. As science moves more to describing the universe as energy, we see ourselves more as energetic beings with a physical form. The Twelve Rays are a particular type of energy that comes directly from the Source and is stepped down for us to experience in this dimension. The Rays have been described as "the clothing for the energy that we are".

Music of the Twelve Rays

Every civilization on the planet uses music. It seems that each generation develops its own expression of popular music. Many cultures also use a specialized type of music in their spiritual rituals to create an altered state of awareness. I have teamed up with Richard Shulman to create a specialized type of music that is infused with the energy of the Twelve Rays. We have recorded this music and offer it on a two-CD release that we have named *A New Awareness*.

Use the music to help you connect with the energy of the Ray that you are working with. It is generally recognized that most individuals have a primary sensory orientation, either auditory, visual, or kinesthetic. This music should be particularly beneficial for those of you with an auditory orientation. Allow the music to help you experience the energy of the Ray.

I enjoy blending the guided journeys that I conduct in these workshops with the music of the Rays. I hope you have the opportunity to experience Richard's live playing during your workshop. When Richard is not available to play live, I will use his recorded music in the workshop.

Artwork of the Twelve Rays

The preceding comments about music are also applicable to art. Every culture has its own art styles and periods. I have teamed up with Melinda Radcliffe to create artwork for each one of the Rays. For those of you with a visual sensory orientation, use the artwork to help you connect with the energy of the Rays.

As a matter of fact, I suggest doing your own meditations using the image of any given Ray. Allow the images and the colors to help you experience at a deeper level the energy of the Rays.

For those individuals who have a primary sensory orientation that is kinesthetic, you get to use all of the above to help you connect to the energy of the Rays.

CHAPTER 1

The Truth

Many of us spend a lot of time as adults trying to change the stories that grownups told us when we were children. Many of these stories where well intended. As a matter of fact, I bet most adults would say that the vast majority of them were for our own good. There are several different groups of stories. Probably the group that does the least amount of damage is the one that covers the cultural holidays. Santa Claus and the Easter Bunny are a couple of well-known examples of this group.

Sooner or later, every child learns that Santa is not real, but strangely enough, knowing that doesn't prevent the gifts from coming. After dealing with the trauma of there being no Santa Claus, the truth about the Easter Bunny is easier to deal with, and again strangely enough, knowing the truth about the Easter Bunny doesn't prevent the chocolate from showing up on Easter morning. The Tooth Fairy comes to mind as do storks dropping babies down chimneys.

I think we probably learn the most half-truths in school. Let's begin with history. Was Columbus really the first one to discover America? And after he discovered America, what became of the inhabitants? Let's just say that the local inhabitants were not treated very kindly by Columbus. He was for a short time arrested and imprisoned for his actions in the new world, but he was later released and, I assume, vindicated.

If you grew up in the United States, your history books never discussed the genocide that the European settlers waged against the native Americans. The American Indians were portrayed as the bad guys, and the United States Calvary was called on to defeat the enemy. The real story seems to be vastly different from what we were taught in school. And at the same time, slavery was a common practice in this new country.

Let's consider science for a moment. Every now and then, scientists come up with a new theory that gets them in trouble with the church. The theory of evolution that was proposed by Charles Darwin is a great example of this. My understanding is that evolution is currently not taught in middle and high schools around the country where the church still has strong control.

These days, Darwin has been challenged by the popular theory that he replaced, which is called epigenetics, which was developed by a Frenchman by the name of Jean-Baptiste Lamarck. Epigenetics explains rapid changes in species in very short timeframes, certainly within the lifetime of a single member of that species. These quick changes are most often the result of environmental changes rather than mutations over long periods of time.

Perhaps the most monumental changes in how we see science has come about through Einstein's Theory of Relativity and quantum physics. I'm not going to even try to get conceptual about relativity or quantum physics. What I do know is that somewhere along the way, scientists developed the theory of dark matter and estimate that it may make up close to 70 percent of the universe. This means that what we learned about space being a vast empty void is simply not true. I might also add that just about everything we learned about atoms is also not true any longer.

Whose Truth

The truth seems to be, at best, a moving target. It seems to me that it is constantly being updated. Sure, you might expect that with the sciences. Technology gets better, and scientists are able to uncover more, see farther, see smaller. How many of us keep up with the scientific discoveries? How many of us still believe that we only use 10 percent of our brains? How many of us still believe that space is empty? If we don't keep current, we still hold those out-of-date beliefs.

What happens when history gets revised? There are those who want to eliminate the national Columbus Day celebration. Many object to this because they still believe he was a great explorer.

Take a look at our current political environment. Many politicians still do not believe in global warming, although almost all scientists do. A large number of voters think that the current president is great. Some portion of voters think just the opposite. Who is right? Where is the truth?

There was a time when I thought that the truth was undeniable. And while it is probably true and always will be true that 2 plus 2 equals 4, such truths are hard to find when it comes to dealing with people and their beliefs. When talking about the truth, I like to picture an image of the sun with rays emanating from all 360 degrees. And I think that each ray represents the truth to someone. What I'm trying to say here is that I think the truth is most often subjective. People seem to find it easy to accept "facts" that support their current beliefs.

Want-to-Believers

What does any of this have to do with this workshop? We were told religious stories about the creation of the universe. They taught us about God and heaven and hell. They taught us that we are sinners and that we need to be forgiven. They taught us that God sent his only son to save us. They taught us that we live only once, and when we die, we are judged.

What if all the stuff we were taught as children about who we are and why we are here were not necessarily false stories but were just framed in an ancient metaphor that doesn't make sense to us anymore?

I was raised in a Catholic household and taught by the nuns in grammar school and the Jesuits in high school. I became an altar boy just like my older brothers. By the time I was ready to graduate from high school, I had left the church far behind.

I tried to find some other belief system that would work for me, but I had little success. Walking away from your family's belief system and values is hard enough. Spending a lot of energy looking for a replacement can be exhausting. I came up with a solution that worked for me at the time. I put the entire matter on the back burner. If there really was a God, I'm sure that at some appropriate time he or she would make themselves known.

And that is exactly what happened. The only problem is that it happened nearly thirty years later. In those intervening thirty years, I more or less felt like I had little direction in my life other than to be successful. I did alright. Had a lovely wife and three children, a nice house, and a relatively well-paying job.

During this thirty-year hiatus, I was a want-to-believer. I wanted to believe in something larger than myself. I wanted to have a crystal-clear moral compass that would guide me in my decision-making. But I didn't have that, so I did the best I could. My moral compass at the time was based on fear. When it was time to make a decision, I would ask myself, "Does this create more fear in my life, or does it reduce the fear that I have?" Things didn't turn out so well for me using fear as my moral compass. I wound up divorced, alone, in a new job that I didn't like, and in a different city that was away from my family. Then things got worse. I'll spare you the details.

Then I crossed paths with the Divine again. I was introduced to New Age thinking. Here was a much more modern metaphor for who we are and why we are here. I wholeheartedly jumped on board the metaphysical bandwagon. I installed a new moral compass. I replaced my fear compass with a new love compass. Every decision was based upon creating more love in my life. I left corporate America behind and opened a New Age wellness center. I had found my new calling. I began working with alternative healing modalities like Reiki and quantum touch. I met all kinds of psychics and readers. And then I met the person who was to change my life forever.

I refer to this individual as Julie in my book. That is not her real name. Julie had a message for me. It had been given to her telepathically by a group of entities from somewhere else whom we refer to as "The Team." The message that she received was that they wanted to talk to us. So we began to have sessions where they would talk to me through Julie. During one of these sessions, I believe it was about the twentieth, they told me they wanted to give us information about the Twelve Rays. We recorded all these sessions, and that is the information that I used to describe the Rays in my book *The Reality of Your Greatness: A Personal Journey through the Twelve Rays.*

I have been working with the Rays for more than ten years. This workshop has evolved over time into its present format. I mentioned earlier that I believe you need three things to get the most out of this workshop. I am now going to add a fourth. I strongly suggest you maintain an open mind about the "truths" that you have learned up till now. Please be willing to consider the possibility that some of the beliefs that you hold as true are really holding you back.

When there was a common belief that the Earth was flat, even though the Greeks had proved that it was round, not many sailors ventured too far into the open sea. The Twelve Rays present many concepts that contradict the dogma that I was raised in as a Catholic. At the same time, they provide many answers that I couldn't find in that 2,000-year-old dogma that I believed.

CHAPTER 2

Practical Applications of the First Three Rays

The conditions that I have focused on in this workbook are ones that anyone could experience on any given day. Resistance to change, stress reduction, loneliness, manifesting your desires, and the Law of Attraction may not seem like your typical medical conditions. They may not be the direct cause of the symptoms that you are experiencing, but you will probably be able to find a connection to your internal problems.

We will be working in this Foundational Workshop with the first three Rays, which are referred to as the Rays of Aspect. The next chapter gives a short overview of all the Rays. Before that overview, let's talk a little bit about what we will be covering today.

The First Ray – Divine Will
Resistance to Change

The first section of the practical applications deals with resistance to change. I am going to go out on a limb here and suggest that we have probably all experienced resistance to change at some point. There are two particular types of resistance to change that we will work with here. The first is called procrastination. Yes, procrastination is a form of resistance to change. By continuing to put something off, you are most often in fact resisting the change that this goal represents.

There is another widespread type of resistance to change that can be called distraction. We hear a lot about distraction in our society today, and it is a proven way to resist change. With all the constant distractions offered by our technology, we don't need to go too far to get totally thrown off of our best intentions. The thing about being distracted is that we most of the time don't even realize we are doing it. The distraction crosses our path, and we take off after it like a dog chasing a squirrel, and then some time later remember that there was something that we were supposed to be doing. What was that again? Too bad. I have to go do this other thing now. Distraction triumphs again.

We use the First Ray to identify the source of the resistance to change. Our desire, of course, is to move beyond the resistance and accomplish the goals that we have set for ourselves. You will see how we use the Third Ray, the Ray of Active Intelligence, to create the plan that gets the job done. The objective here is to simply identify the source of the resistance.

Stress Reduction

Stress reduction can be effectively achieved using the First Ray. We all have stressors in our lives. Some of them are very purposeful. The useful stressors can influence us to take action, for example. But there are many stressors that don't serve us at all. Some of these are beliefs from earlier personal experiences. Some are just flat out imaginary. Others can just come from bad habits that we have developed along the way. There are plenty of these unnecessary stressors in everyone's life, and we can use the First Ray in much the same way as we do with identifying resistance to change to help us identify the stressors. Then we can use the Third Ray to create a plan to move beyond the particular stressor by changing the belief about it.

There are three different scenarios that I present in the stress reduction section. The first is stress that arises from past personal experience. I use the example of fear of flying. Why are some people afraid of flying, heights, water, or you name it? It is because they have had a personal experience with it, which led them to a new belief, a belief that flying is dangerous, etc. We can use the First Ray to identify that past personal experience and change the belief that was created back then to something that takes the stress out of it.

A second source of stress is what I refer to as scarcity stress. This involves the belief that there is not enough of something—not enough money, food, or even hours in the day. The truth is that there is enough of all of those, and you can use the First Ray to change your belief about scarcity.

The third source of stress that we will cover is future stress. This is simply stressing over something in the future that has not even happened yet. Many individuals have vivid imaginations and can conjure up all sorts of stressful future scenarios. While there may have been a time in your life that this was a necessary survival strategy, it probably is no longer necessary. But if it still is required for survival, then there are bigger issues to deal with right now.

The Second Ray – Love and Wisdom
Moving Beyond Loneliness

The Second Ray is the Ray of Love and Wisdom, and it can be particularly helpful in working with individuals who are feeling lonely and disconnected. As it turns out, loneliness is a human emotion. What I mean by that is loneliness does not exist in the higher dimensions.

The illusion of separation from our higher self, our whole self, creates what I refer to as Spiritual Discord. I think of this as the spiritual side of physical birth trauma. The need to work with any individual's Spiritual Discord varies from person to person and is really not part of this workshop. However, it is often very beneficial work. I will certainly write more about this soon.

One of the most dramatic characteristics of this dimension is this illusion of separation, this illusion that we are stand-alone individuals, separated from each other. There is great purpose in this illusion since it does not, as I just pointed out, exist in the higher realms.

We come here knowing that the experience of loneliness is practically unavoidable, but we don't have to let it overwhelm us. We can remember our connection to our whole selves, and we can remember that in actuality, we have never been cut off from our whole selves or from Divine Love. Some individuals allow loneliness to be a bigger part of their human experience than others and can greatly benefit from working with the Second Ray to remember their connection.

If the source of the loneliness stems from the loss of something—a loved one, human or animal, or a lifestyle like a career, a home, or a marriage, or even the loss of a favorite pastime or hobby—then these are all special cases, and a personalized solution has to be tailored to each individual. When you introduce a bigger picture, you can gain a different perspective and this is sure to help in most every circumstance, but you'll most likely need more than just that.

The Third Ray – Active Intelligence
Manifesting Your Desires

I've already mentioned that we use the Third Ray, the Ray of Active Intelligence in connection with the First Ray. Once we have identified the source of the resistance to change or the source of the stress in our lives, we use this Third Ray to help us define the steps we need to take to manifest our new beliefs. When we put all the steps together, we have a nice, simple plan to follow.

Resistance to change and stress reduction are two special cases that I have singled out because they are so pervasive in our society today. As such, a broad spectrum of individuals can be helped by using this approach. I think that makes them very practical.

The Law of Attraction

The more general approach can be referred to as the Law of Attraction. I like the approach that Neville Goddard used to teach. In case you are not familiar with Goddard, Wayne Dyer talks about him at length in his book *Wishes Fulfilled*. Goddard has a four-step formula that makes it very easy to get good results.

There are several books that have recently popularized the Law of Attraction. From my perspective, it seems as though the Law of Attraction doesn't work for most people. There are many possible reasons for this lack of success. One of perhaps the most pervasive reasons is simply a lack of focus. I'll talk more about that in the upcoming section.

Personal beliefs also account for a huge part of the lack of success with the Law of Attraction. Let me give you a simple example. If you believe that money is the root of all evil, then trying to use the Law of Attraction to become rich is very understandably going to be difficult for you. The Law of Attraction is not going to override your core beliefs about yourself and the world. You have to change your personal beliefs first by yourself. Just as an aside, the Seventh Ray is a great tool to help you do that.

Get Creative

The specific examples that I have just outlined and that are detailed in the remainder of this workbook are just that. They are specific examples. There is probably no limitation on the number of ways that the Twelve Rays can be used for your personal benefit. The more you work with them, the more familiar you will become with them. This will help you to build your confidence and encourage you to make them your own.

As I mentioned earlier, these first three Rays are our Divine Inheritance. Most have never heard of them before or perhaps never thought of them in this way before. There are many different philosophies and religious ideologies that have helped to shape the world as we know it today. Some of them are uplifting, while others hold us back. Some invite us to find our own paths, while others teach us to defend their dogma.

It is probably going to take a significant amount of work for most people to embrace and own the Divinity within them. It wasn't easy for me to do, and I don't think I'm that different than most people in that regard. For so long we have been bombarded with messages that we are less than, that we are broken and need to be fixed, that we need a savior. The Twelve Rays are a message of healing and hope. They are a modern metaphor that helps us explain and understand who we are in this modern, digital age.

Most change doesn't happen overnight. We need to have patience with ourselves and with those around us. Participating in this workshop is a great way to help us all move forward.

Let's have a quick overview of the Twelve Rays before we begin looking at some specific examples of using the first three Rays.

The Twelve Rays offer a new cosmology, a new explanation of how the universe was created and why it was created. They offer us a new understanding of who we are and why we are here on this planet in this universe.

– MICHAEL LOVE

CHAPTER 3

The Twelve Rays as Metaphor

The Twelve Rays represent a metaphor of the origin of the universe and humankind's relationship with a Divine Creator that is in line with our current understanding of how things work in our modern, digital world. This metaphor uses energy to describe the basic nature of both God and all of creation. It is offered as an update to the historical mythologies of previous eras.

Think of the Twelve Rays then as not so much a new truth that is being revealed to humankind, but a more up-to-date metaphor of the creation story and humankind's place within this universe.

The story of Abraham obeying God's command to sacrifice his son Isaac fits the cultural mythology of the day. The understanding that a single God was responsible for both the joy and the sorrow in the world completely justified the necessity to make offerings to God to incur his blessings. Most of the time, an animal was sufficient for the offering. But in Abraham's case, God tested him by saying that his only son needed to be sacrificed. Thankfully, it didn't come to that. A ram was provided instead.

Fast forward a couple of thousand years, and the prevailing cultural mythology was accepting of a savior to deliver the people of Israel. While Jesus wasn't successful in delivering the Jews from Roman occupation, he was credited with saving his followers from their sins. This concept was part of the old Jewish yearly ritual of putting their sins on the back of a goat and sending that goat out into the desert. This is where our current notion of a scapegoat comes from.

In the twenty-first century, the notion of a literal savior to deliver his people from oppressive foreign rule is not something that resonates in Western society.

Renowned author and scholar Joseph Campbell came to the conclusion that our current Western cultural mythology is, however, broken. In examining cultural mythologies from around the world, Campbell came to the conclusion that cultural mythologies have four key functions. I am going to paraphrase them below:

1. The first function of a living mythology is the mystical function. It opens up a realization of the mystical dimension. It says that behind the everyday aspects of life, there is a transcendent mystery that is the source of life, and that source is also within you.
2. The second function of mythology is to present an image of the cosmos that will maintain your sense of mystic awe and explain everything that you come into contact with in the universe around you.
3. The third function of a mythological order is to validate and maintain a certain sociological system: a shared set of rights and wrongs, proprieties or improprieties, on which your particular social unit depends for its existence.
4. The fourth function is psychological. The myth must carry the individual through the stages of his life, from birth through maturity through senility to death.

Campbell believed that the scientific revolution corrupted the Judeo-Christian cosmology. The first crack came with Galileo and his claim that the Earth revolved around the Sun. Next came Darwin and his book *The Origins of Species*. It is easy to see how this upset the claim of the universe being created by God.

The Twelve Rays offer a new cosmology, a new explanation of how the universe was created and why it was created. They offer us a new understanding of who we are and why we are here on this planet in this universe. In addition, they offer a new moral compass by which we can learn how to live together in peace and harmony.

I am not suggesting that the Rays are the only way or even a better way to describe what has been described in the past. I am saying that I believe them to be a more up-to-date and perhaps more relevant explanation for our current times and our collective understanding of life here in this dimension. That being said, let me provide a short overview of the Twelve Rays for your review.

Overview of the Twelve Rays

(excerpt from *The Reality of Your Greatness:*
A Personal Journey through the Twelve Rays)

The Twelve Rays can be divided into three separate groups: the Rays
of Aspect, the Rays of Attributes, and the Rays of Soul Integration.
The first three Rays are referred to as the Rays of Aspect. They are the

three aspects of the Creator that are filtered down through the various levels of creation before they enter into our dimension. They are filtered even further within our universe. Our physical bodies are not capable of receiving the full intensities of the Rays. The First Ray, the Ray of Divine Will, is filtered through the bear constellation known as Ursa Major. The Second Ray, the Ray of Love and Wisdom, is filtered through the triune star system Sirius, which is in the constellation known as Canis Major, the big dog. The Third Ray, the Ray of Active Intelligence, is filtered through the Pleiades. Each of these three areas acts as a focal point within our universe. They then direct the energy of the Rays to Earth.

The next group of Rays is known as the Rays of Attributes. They enable us to take on the multitude of human characteristics that provide us with the life experiences that are unique to this dimension. This group includes the Fourth Ray, the Ray of Harmony through Conflict; the Fifth Ray, the Ray of Concrete Knowledge; the Sixth Ray, the Ray of Devotion and Idealism; and the Seventh Ray, which is known by a few names. The Team refers to the Seventh Ray as the Gateway into Awareness. I generally refer to it as the Violet Flame.

The Rays of Aspect and the Rays of Attributes comprise the first Seven Rays and have been written about and taught for hundreds of years. Alice Bailey wrote about the Rays extensively in her book *The Rays and the Initiations*, which was published in 1960. It is interesting to note that she only discusses the first seven Rays in that publication.

The Rays of Soul Integration, Rays Eight through Twelve, have only become available within the last forty years or so. For those of you who are also interested in astrology, it is interesting to note that this roughly corresponds with the first observation of Chiron. According to Barbara Hand Clow in her book *Chiron: Rainbow Bridge Between the Inner and Outer Planets*, "Chiron is the teacher of the Earth connection to higher planes, and the planetary sighting indicates the time has come for us to manifest our divinity." There are two ways that the Rays help us to do that. One is by embracing our Divine Inheritance. The other is through soul integration.

Soul integration is a process now available to all of humankind. I will have much more to share about soul integration in the coming chapters. It is important to understand that Rays Eight through Twelve are the tools given to us to achieve soul integration.

The Team refers to the Eighth Ray as the Cleansing Ray, and it is used in conjunction with the Seventh Ray. The Ninth Ray, the Ray of Contact with the Soul Level, is used to connect with the higher aspects of self. The Tenth Ray is the Ray of the Body of Light and will be discussed extensively later. The Eleventh Ray is the Bridge to New Awareness. Before I discuss the New Awareness, let me point out that the Twelfth

Ray is the New Awareness. I can't give you a definition of what the New Awareness is. I believe it is different for each individual. My hope is that by the end of this book, you will be able to tell me what your New Awareness is.

Each Ray represents a certain energetic frequency. This frequency is also symbolized by a color or a color pattern. Some Rays are a single color, while others are a blend of colors since they are a blend of Rays. The color of the individual Rays will be given as each Ray is introduced.

Julie and I were introduced to the Rays one Ray at a time. My sense of why it was done that way is that it gave us time to process and incorporate the frequency of each individual Ray separately. My recommendation is that, as you read about the Rays, you allow time in between each one to work with the exercises that are given. This will allow you to integrate each Ray into your physical structure.

Working with the Rays takes you on a journey that involves permanently raising your energetic level as you go. There is no shortcut available. You will not be able to work with the higher Rays if you have not properly integrated the lower Rays into your energetic field. If at any time during your journey you find that the next Ray is for some reason blocked or you are not able to access it, ask yourself if you have really taken the time to integrate the preceding Ray's energies. It is a simple task to go back and repeat a step or two.

It is up to you to do the work. I hope that you have had experience with meditation in the past. If not, don't worry. You can go to the Twelve Rays website and access free, guided meditations that will help you to become familiar with this very empowering self-practice. All the guided meditations presented in this book are also available on that website.

The answers that you are looking for are inside you. The path to the inner dimensions is inside you. The support that you need to accomplish whatever it is that you choose to achieve is accessible within you. Journeying inside, since at one time or another it is new to all of us, can be a daunting endeavor. Going where you have never gone before is often a challenge. We all enjoy maintaining the status quo. But there is something that compels us to move forward, to start the journey down a new road. You will be rewarded for your effort.

The preceding overview is meant to be only an introduction. Much more information about the Rays is available within the book.

The Twelve Rays offer not only a set of tools to help on your personal life journeys, they also provide a new, modern metaphor of what mankind's roles and capabilities are now and in the future in this physical dimension.

– MICHAEL LOVE

CHAPTER 4

Working with the Rays

You may find working with the Rays to be a little different than what you are normally used to. The specific areas that we will be working with in this workshop are experiences that almost everyone has. They typically don't seem like big deals, and I'm willing to bet that you haven't sought outside help for relief of loneliness, for example.

The way I see it, loneliness is a component of many conditions that many individuals experience. And I believe that it is totally normal to feel lonely under certain conditions. However, loneliness can become chronic and, when left unattended, could possibly develop into serious issues like depression. It is estimated that over 16 million people in the United States alone have a major depressive experience at least once a year. We know that anti-depressants are widely prescribed and that they often become habit forming.

Helping people to cope with their periods of loneliness might just help to bring down the number of people who experience a yearly depressive event. And that might help to reduce the volume of antidepressants that are prescribed and taken.

If working with loneliness might help to prevent some episodes of depression, could it have benefits in other areas? How about reducing stress? Certainly, if you feel loved and supported, it would have a very positive effect on your stress level! I'm sure you can think about the positive effects of reducing loneliness in other areas.

One of the things that we will be talking about throughout this entire workshop is what our present understanding of disease is. When I say our, I mean yours and mine. I'm not going to suggest that any one understanding of the word "disease" is better than any other. I am going to share with you that my understanding of that word has constantly evolved over time.

Let me go deeper into this sense of how working with the energy of the

Rays might be different for you. These first three Rays are really about personal empowerment, but most individuals don't even know that the Rays are theirs to use and command. Once it becomes clear that these first Rays are for everyone, that they are indeed our Divine Heritage, then it is safe to assume that resistance will kick in sooner or later. Let me share with you something from Steven Pressfield's *The War of Art:*

> *These are serious fears. But they are not the real fear. Not the Master Fear, the Mother of all Fears that's so close to us that even when we verbalize it, we don't believe it.*
> *Fear That We Will Succeed.*
> *That we can access the powers we secretly know we possess.*
> *That we can become the person we sense in our hearts we truly are. ...*
> *We fear discovering that we are more than we think we are.*

When you begin learning about the Rays, you can gain the perspective that you are more than what you think you are. When you learn about your Divine Heritage, if you are at all like me, most likely sooner or later you will experience resistance. And that is why working with other forms of resistance to change is so important. If you are uncomfortable with the smaller changes that you encounter, then asking you to process the Rays is going to be difficult.

As you begin to work with the next group of Rays, the Rays of Attributes, the Seventh Ray, what we used to call the Violet Flame and now call the Gateway to Awareness, will be invaluable in transmuting "the weightiness of past experience." We use the Seventh Ray to process our baggage that we are carrying with us. These past experiences all have emotional baggage associated with them. It is not our intention to forget these experiences, but rather to transmute the lower-level emotions associated with them like fear, anger, shame, etc., into a higher level of acceptance and forgiving. There will be more on this in the seminar on the Rays of Attributes.

The entire purpose of working with the Rays can be viewed as a journey to a higher level of consciousness, which also involves a higher energetic level of being. Any individual who is working with the Rays needs to do enough work to raise their own personal energetic levels to such a degree that allows them to work with the new, higher-level Rays. The Rays are self-regulating. You won't be successful with the higher ones until you have done your own work.

The new Rays, the Rays of Soul Integration, require a certain personal energetic level in order to use them. I can't tell you exactly what that level is. What I can do is help you to achieve that level. The Rays of Soul Integration are really the tools to help humankind advance to the next level of existence here in this physical dimension. The opportunity that they represent is truly amazing. After helping us to establish contact with our individual soul levels, the Tenth Ray allows us to begin to anchor our Body of Light into this dimension. The implications of this are simply transformational. All of this will be covered in the Rays of Soul Integration workshop.

I hope this brief discussion has given you some idea of what to expect when you work with the techniques that are presented in these workshops.

Resistance is the most toxic force on the planet. It is the root of more unhappiness than poverty, disease, and erectile dysfunction. To yield to Resistance deforms our spirit. It stunts us and makes us less than we are and were born to be.

- STEVEN PRESSFIELD,
The War of Art: Break Through the Blocks & Win Your Inner Creative Battles

CHAPTER 5

The First Ray
Divine Will
Resistance to Change

Ever hear the saying "change is good"? It is easy to agree with that statement. I think in reality, though, most of us don't really believe it. Many of us struggle with change and often expend a fair amount of energy trying to avoid it. There is another saying: "The only thing that is certain is change." We seem to have this paradoxical mindset that although change is good and most likely unavoidable, we still work hard to resist it.

Change is risky, and many of us don't like taking risks. When we pursue change, we are unsure of the outcome. We have an anticipation of how the change will affect us, but there really is no guarantee that our desired outcome will be the same as the actual outcome. Is it any wonder that we often ask ourselves if the change is worth the risk and decide to do nothing instead?

Even when we decide that a certain change would most definitely benefit us, we still often find it hard to embrace. Why is that I wonder? When we know that changing jobs could be the best thing in the world for us, we stay put. When we know that a current relationship isn't working out, we tell ourselves that it is better than being alone. When we know that there is something we could do that would change our lives for the better, we choose to not take any action. What is it about us that makes it so comfortable to just continue on the way we are?

Change Is Hard

Could there be something inside us that is actually working to prevent change? There are many different explanations about why change seems to be so difficult. We all have our favorite things to do, and when we do them day in and day out, they become patterns. There is a pattern to what you do in the morning once you get out of bed. There is a pattern in how you drive to your place of employment. There is probably a pattern in your daily work routine. There are all kinds of patterns, and when we do them over and over, they become repetitive patterns or habits.

Most of our habits are really very beneficial. They actually are a way to optimize our brain power since most of our habits are so ingrained that they require very little conscious focusing. This apparent benefit might actually have a little bit of a down side. We can accumulate so many repetitive patterns that we actually do very little thinking during our waking moments. We don't have to pay as much attention when we are doing our repetitive patterns. We almost don't know that we are even doing them.

What does this have to do with embracing change? It takes effort to change. We have to stop an existing pattern, and we have to create a new pattern. Let's use an example. Say you want to change how you commute to work every day. Suppose you drive to work by yourself, and you think it would be better to use mass transit because it is better for the environment. Instead of simply hopping in your car and driving to work, you either walk or drive to the train station, park if you drove, get a ticket, and wait for the train. Then once on board, you have to find a seat, which you most likely will share with a total stranger. When you get to your destination, you still have to walk to your place of employment. You ask yourself, "Is this really worth it?" The point is, it takes a lot of effort to change, and it takes no effort to continue in our established patterns.

Forms of Resistance to Change

Let's change this example just a little bit. Say you want to start taking the train to your work every day, but you just never really seem to be able to make the change. For some reason, you just never seem to be able to start the new routine. You are most likely encountering some form of resistance. The thing about resistance to change is that it is often difficult to spot the source of the resistance.

Very often a person doesn't even recognize that there is resistance. They know they want to change something, but they just never seem to get around to it. "Oh, I'll start that next week," they say to themselves. This is a specialized form of resistance called procrastination. You keep putting something off, and you just never seem to get around to it. But there is something that is causing this procrastination, and we need to figure out what it is in order to get on with the change.

Take a few minutes and think about how procrastination works with other issues. How about relationships? Often, we let failing relationships drag on way too long because we fear the change. The same can be said of careers. How often have individuals stayed in a job that was going nowhere instead of taking action to find that next positive career move? I know I've stayed in certain jobs way too long! Moving your residence, finishing your educational goals, writing that book, the list goes on and on.

There is another specialized form of resistance that is called distraction. You set your intention to start something new, and then you get distracted by something else, in many cases anything else, and then you are totally sidetracked. This can quite normally happen without you actually becoming aware of it. Once you are involved with the distraction, you can totally forget what it was you were wanting to do. It could be hours or even days later when you realize that you got distracted. Again, there is a reason why you are being distracted, and if you ever want to really change, you have to figure out what that reason is.

Discovering the Sources of Resistance

As it turns out, resistance to change is often a successful strategy for maintaining the status quo. Deciding to make change in our personal lives can have dramatic consequences, so we should exercise caution when evaluating the benefits and the risks. However, as I discussed earlier, life is all about change, and using discernment to evaluate what to embrace and what to leave alone is always appropriate.

I wish I could tell you that your fear of changing how you travel to work every day is related to a fear of _____ (fill in the blank). There are dozens of possible things that a normal person could feel uneasy about. Let's start with a fear of giving up control. If you take the train, you are not driving the train. Could be a fear of falling and hurting yourself. Could be a fear of strangers. The list goes on and on. I wish I could tell you which one of these is causing your resistance, but I can't. I can, however, share with you how to go about finding the answer.

When you look at the magnitude of disease in the world today, the number of individuals with cancer, heart disease, hypertension, diabetes, depression, and so on, you wonder why some individuals get better and others don't. Could it be that the ones who aren't getting better are resisting the changes that are necessary to regain their health?

Let's get to the source of the resistance. The resistance is coming from inside you. In order to find the root cause of the resistance then, it is necessary to journey within. One of the best ways to do that is through meditation. There are all different kinds of meditation. I'm not suggesting anything very exotic. For our purposes here, meditation is not a whole lot more than just taking ten to twenty minutes and quieting yourself so that you can hear that inner voice that you have that holds so many answers to your personal questions.

Before you begin the following exercise, take a few minutes and think about the areas of resistance to change that you want to work with. Then pick one and write it down below. You need clarity here, so please be as specific as possible.

In this exercise I will be working on resistance to change in the following area:

_____

_____

_____

The following is a guided journey, my version of a meditation, that I use with my clients when I am particularly interested in getting to the source of resistance. In this guided journey, I am going to ask you to focus your attention on two things. First, focus on the thing that you are trying to change/heal. And as you focus on it, formulate the question, "What is the source of the resistance that is preventing me from moving forward, from healing?" Remember that we are only looking to identify the source of the resistance. Creating a plan to move beyond the resistance is a separate step.

The second thing I am going to ask you to focus on is the First Ray, the Ray of Divine Will. And just to refresh your memory, this Ray is a beautiful red color and is part of our Divine Heritage. We use this Ray to think about what we want to create in our lives. And when we experience resistance to actually manifesting what we desire, we use this Ray to identify the source of the resistance.

When you are ready to proceed with this guided journey, read through it once. Then you can decide to either read it again into a recording device like your phone, or you can go to my website thetwelverays.com, and listen to the audio file that I have recorded. Here is the guided journey.

Meditation: IDENTIFYING RESISTANCE USING THE FIRST RAY

Let's begin by taking a gentle, deep breath. Gently inhale and then slowly exhale. With each breath in, breathe in fresh, relaxing air, and with each exhale, breathe out any stress or tension you may be feeling. You may close your eyes if you find that more relaxing. Please make sure your feet are firmly on the floor if you are sitting. Feel free to sit with your legs folded underneath you if that is more familiar to you. Allow your hands to gently relax in your lap or at your side. Now take another gentle, deep breath and again gently exhale and become more and more relaxed.

Now imagine in your mind's eye, using your inner vision, your favorite place to go and relax. You may see yourself in a fishing boat in the middle of a serene lake. Or perhaps you see yourself sunbathing at the beach. Perhaps you are sitting on a rock in the mountains that overlooks a beautiful, lush valley. Maybe you are relaxing in your favorite chair in your home. I like to see myself floating on my back in a crystal clear, spring-fed grotto. We all have a place in our minds where we can go and relax and feel safe and secure and peaceful.

In this place, let's call it your sacred place, you might sense the presence of those who look out for you from beyond this dimension. We sometimes recognize these helpers as loved ones who have passed. Sometimes we see them as angels. Some call them teachers; some call them guides. When you are nice and comfortable, you may wish to call in your loved ones or your guides and teachers if you normally meditate with them. You might choose to call in your angels instead. If you don't normally connect with any other entities during your meditations, it is fine to just be by yourself. That's right, nice and relaxed, feeling very comfortable.

I would like you to think about the power of your thoughts. Thoughts are powerful things. Think of the last time you attended a conference, a meeting, a concert, or actually any event. That decision to attend the event started with a thought. Some piece of information, maybe an invitation in the mail or an advertisement someplace, on television or on the radio or on the Internet, created a thought, "Would this be of interest for me?" Then you started evaluating the pros and the cons and eventually came to a decision, and that decision led you to take action, and that is how you wound up attending the event. It all started with that first thought.

If you think about it, many of the experiences we have had in our lives came about roughly the same way. It starts with the thought. But not all thoughts result in action. Some of them get stuck along the way. Sometimes we find it hard to make a choice. When this happens, you may be experiencing resistance. There is something deeper that is putting the brakes on the whole process. This is how we can use the First Ray to help us identify the source of the resistance to change.

Now I would like you to visualize a beautiful, red light above your head. Allow this red light—this rich, vibrant light—to represent the energy of the First Ray. Invite the First Ray to begin to penetrate your energetic field. Allow it to descend down toward the top of your head. Now allow the First Ray to begin to move through your body. Allow it to move past your head, surrounding you with a column of lush, vibrant, red light. Allow it to continue to move down. See it now surrounding your abdomen. Allow it to move past your waist and down through your legs. Allow it to continue down into your feet and even farther, flowing down into Mother Earth.

This is the energy of the First Ray, Divine Will, directed down through the layers of creation into our solar system through the many levels of your being. It is an energy of change, of allowing. When you invoke the First Ray, you step from that point of sameness onto the path of evolution and change.

Your recognition of Divine Will was the beginning of self, for with that recognition was born thought, and with thought, self was born. Divine Will is an allowance, a gift to go and create, to design, to define this self that you recognize.

Divine Will is a characteristic of a higher consciousness, the drive and determination beyond the ego. It is a characteristic of the warrior, and you will find it helpful when great change has taken place. It comes to you through your soul, stepping down into your personality, into your atomic structure, and helps bring greater awareness and vision to the larger picture.

Allow yourself to claim the role of creator of your own reality. You have the power to create your life any way you choose. Remember that all of your current life experiences have brought you to this moment when you claim your power as creator of your own reality.

(Pause one minute.)

Recall the goal that you decided to work with today. Call on this energy, this Divine Will, whenever you are feeling less than the light that you are, whenever you feel paralyzed to choose the direction you know in your heart points you to the light, the greater, more expanded, brighter light. Allow this energy of the First Ray to make you aware of any resistance to moving forward and achieving your goal. Allow it to show you the source of the resistance. Don't worry about how you might move beyond the resistance for now. We simply want to identify where the resistance is coming from. Take a minute and allow the awareness to come.

(Pause one minute.)

In a minute we will begin our journey back. Use this remaining time to communicate with your guides and teachers or any other entities who might have joined you today. Ask them if they have anything else to share with you today. Thank them for their continued help and guidance. Thank them for being here with you today.

When you are ready to return, begin your journey back by taking a gentle, deep breath. Slowly exhale, and as you do, begin to feel your fingers and your toes and begin to gently move them. As you begin to wiggle your fingers and your toes, allow your consciousness to begin to fully return to your physical body. As you feel your consciousness fully returning to your physical body, become aware of your arms and your legs. And when you are ready, gently open your eyes and return to this place and this time. Welcome back.

Take some time and write down the insights that you have received. If you don't have a clear understanding of the source of your resistance to change, that is fine. Just be on the lookout for some indication or understanding to unfold that may share light on the cause. Not everyone gets an answer the first time. It may take more than one attempt, or it may simply come to you later.

_____

_____

_____

_____

The point of this exercise is to identify the source of the resistance. This information is readily available if we take the time and connect with our inner wisdom. Once you have established the source of the resistance, move on to the Third Ray to create the plan to move beyond the resistance. The complete plan should also include the steps needed along with any resources needed.

My preference is to do this second step in a subsequent session. This allows time for you to process all the information that you received during your session.

Technique: IDENTIFYING RESISTANCE TO CHANGE

Personal Issues
Can't make progress with desired goals.
Don't know why things are so hard.
Never seem to get things done.
Want to change, but for some reason never get around to it.
Have an identified physical condition that is not getting better.

Desired Outcome
End the frustration and achieve the goal.
Feel better about yourself.
Move on.

Key Concepts
External and internal problems.
Most things involve change.
Many reasons to avoid change.
Most answers are within.
Identify the resistance to change.

Process
Focus on one particular goal that you want to achieve.
Keeping focus on that one goal, complete the guided journey using the First Ray.
Remember to only identify what the resistance to change is.

Desired Outcomes
You understand what the resistance to change is and why it is present.
You want to move forward to the next step with the Third Ray.

Undesired Outcomes
No answers were found. *(Suggestion: repeat the process. Resistance is still powerful.)*

No discussion of lifestyles and wellness would be complete without mentioning stress-reduction. In my experience, the most effective method for reducing stress is meditation because it allows us, even without conscious awareness, to reduce emotions that are stuck in modes that subvert a healthy mind-body flow of biochemicals.

– CANDACE B. PERT,
Molecules of Emotion: The Science Behind Mind-Body Medicine

CHAPTER 6

The First Ray Divine Will Stress Reduction

Stress management and stress reduction are two different things. We all experience temporary periods of high stress. We are facing some deadline at work, we have house guests, or someone is sick and needs our attention. There are numerous scenarios that temporarily create stressful situations for us all. Stress management is very helpful in those situations. What I am talking about here is the day-in day-out stress that we all encounter. Here are a few examples:

- Worrying about what other people think about you.
- Worrying about making a fool of yourself.
- Worrying that you will be left all alone in this world.

These are just a few common examples. How do we go about reducing these types of stressors?

Take a minute and think about what exactly stress is. It is your reaction to the world around you. You have choice. What stresses me and what stresses you are probably totally different things. Our stressors are determined in part by our life experiences and our beliefs. Here is an example. Say you are on an airplane flying somewhere, and during the flight the plane encounters some unexpected turbulence. If you are a seasoned traveler, it is likely that you will pay little attention to the bumps and the shaking. Happens all the time. However, if you are not an experienced traveler or don't feel comfortable flying, this turbulence will probably really stress you out. Two different people are experiencing the same event and are having two different reactions to it.

Where do these different reactions come from? They come from personal beliefs. The seasoned traveler has a belief that flying is safe. The nervous traveler may have any one of several different beliefs about flying: flying is unsafe; I'm not in control, and I need to be; this is too much for me to handle, etc. And where do these beliefs come from? They come from past, personal experience.

Think about what stresses you out. What is your belief that is at the heart of the stress? If you want to reduce your stress, then you need to change that belief.

Scarcity Stress

Stress is also often a result of believing in some sort of scarcity. There is a lack of something like money or time or assistance. Let's begin with money. The amount of money that any individual or family has available to them varies dramatically. You see some individuals who make large sums of money and claim to be poor, and conversely, some on very modest incomes have money in the bank. So the issue is not how much money, necessarily, but rather how you use it. In many cases, you can resolve the money issues by either earning more of it or spending less of it.

But there is also your individual belief about money. Is money really the root of all evil? It is interesting to note that the scripture verse where this comes from is really, "The love of money is the root of all evil." The point is, what is your belief about money? If you have a negative view of money, then it is going to be difficult for you to accumulate more of it. So your belief about money is actually the source of your stress and creates the scarcity of money. Change your belief about money and see what happens!

Have you ever heard someone say, "There just never seems to be enough time?" This is also more than likely a belief issue. We all experience the exact amount of time in each and every day. Some people are stressed out by it, and others aren't. The source of this belief is often a boundaries issue. Many people have difficulty understanding what is theirs to do and what is for others to do. This may be at work doing someone else's job for them. It could be at home, preferring to do it yourself rather than getting the appropriate person to do the task.

There are, of course, other sources of the belief that there is never enough time. The thing to remember is that for some people, there is plenty of time. And I would suggest that if certain individuals can successfully manage their time, anyone can do it. Remember that by adjusting the boundaries, you can reduce your individual workload and significantly reduce your stress.

The third case I mentioned is never getting any help. While it is certainly true that some people don't have individuals around them who want to help, it is also certainly true that others either don't ask for assistance or think that they have to do it themselves if they want the job done right. I hope you see where I am going with this. These are, again, personal beliefs that can be changed. And if they are changed, then the stress that goes along with having too much to do will be reduced because you are actually getting help.

Future Stress

One of the major sources of stress is the future. That's right, the future. One of the wonderful talents that humans have is the ability to use our imaginations. It can help us anticipate events in the future and be prepared for them. Not only was this a valuable asset for our ancestors, by helping an individual avoid becoming some predator's next meal, but also it is most helpful to us as modern representatives of the species. It allows us to create multiple choices and then choose from among them, including practical stuff like which route to take to get home after work today to avoid the traffic delays.

We also use our imaginations to create possible scenarios for future events. See if this sounds familiar. You receive an unexpected email from your boss today, and she wants to meet with you first thing in the morning about the current project that you are working on. You create a couple of different scenarios in your head. Either she wants to congratulate you on the great work that you have been doing, or she found out about the latest delay that some other group in your organization just blindsided you with. You choose which is the most likely scenario. If you choose the one with the delay, then you pretty much assume that she is not happy with you. So you better be prepared to explain yourself and have a plan to correct things.

On your drive home, you play out tomorrow's meeting in your head over and over again. The stress begins to build. You may even wake up in the middle of the night thinking about it. Gosh, this is really stressful. And then when you finally sit down with her the next morning after your third cup of coffee, you find out that there is a totally new project coming up that she just wanted you to be aware of. She asks politely about your current project. You tell her you have it under control, and the meeting is over. But all that stress that you have been experiencing the last twenty-four hours was all made up and really served no purpose.

I'm not suggesting that you stop using your imagination. What I am suggesting is that you use it wisely. If you are going to prepare yourself for possible bad outcomes, once you have identified them, then just let them be. There is probably nothing you can do about it at the present time. You might want to prepare some positive outcomes. And again, just let them be. Spend your time being in the present moment. This will relieve a lot of stress about future events.

Are there other sources of stress? There are probably hundreds or thousands of different sources of stress. The point to remember is that you can pretty much control the stress in your life.

Stress as a Motivator

Some people believe that stress is a good motivator. Have you ever heard someone say, "I do my best work when I'm stressed?" What they are really saying is that they are letting stress create their motivation. We have all read that stress takes a tremendous toll on the body. Without going into the details, sustained stress really is bad. My suggestion is that if you are a person who is motivated by stress, then you would do well to retrain yourself to find another source of motivation.

Before you begin the following exercise, take a few minutes and think about the areas of stress reduction that you want to work with. Then pick one and write it down below. You need clarity here so please be as specific as possible.

In this exercise I will be working on stress reduction in the following area:

_____

_____

_____

_____

When you are ready to proceed with this guided journey, read through it once. Then you can decide to either read it again into a recording device like your phone or a digital recorder or you can go to my website, thetwelverays.com, and listen to the audio file that I have recorded. Here is the guided journey.

Meditation: STRESS REDUCTION

We are going to use the First Ray to help us identify the source of our stress. You will notice that this meditation is very similar to the fear of change meditation. And like the fear of change meditation, we are only looking to identify the source of the stress. We will use the Third Ray meditation to create the plan to move beyond the source of the stress.

Let's begin by taking a gentle, deep breath. Gently inhale and then slowly exhale. With each breath in, breathe in fresh, relaxing air, and with each exhale, breathe out any stress or tension you may be feeling. You may close your eyes if you find that more relaxing. Please make sure your feet are firmly on the floor if you are sitting. Feel free to sit with your legs folded underneath you if that is more familiar to you. Allow your hands to gently relax in your lap or at your side. Now take another gentle, deep breath and again gently exhale and become more and more relaxed.

Now imagine in your mind's eye, using your inner vision, your favorite place to go and relax. You may see yourself in a fishing boat in the middle of a serene lake. Or perhaps you see yourself sunbathing at the beach. Perhaps you are sitting on a rock in the mountains that overlooks a beautiful, lush valley. Maybe you are relaxing in your favorite chair in your home. I like to see myself floating on my back in a crystal clear, spring-fed grotto. We all have a place in our minds where we can go and relax and feel safe and secure and peaceful.

In this place, let's call it your sacred place, you might sense the presence of those who look out for you from beyond this dimension. We sometimes recognize these helpers as loved ones who have passed. Sometimes we see them as angels. Some call them teachers; some call them guides. When you are nice and comfortable, you may wish to call in your loved ones or your guides and teachers if you normally meditate with them. You might choose to call in your angels instead. If you don't normally connect with any other entities during your meditations, it is fine to just be by yourself. That's right, nice and relaxed, feeling very comfortable.

Now I would like you to visualize a beautiful, red light above your head. Allow this red light—this rich, vibrant light—to represent the energy of the First Ray. Invite the First Ray to begin to penetrate your energetic field. Allow it to descend down toward the top of your head. Now allow the First Ray to begin to move through your body. Allow it to move past your head, surrounding you like a column of lush, vibrant, red light. Allow it to continue to move down. See it now surrounding your abdomen. Allow it to move past your waist and down through your legs. Allow it to continue down into your feet and even farther, flowing down into Mother Earth.

This is the energy of the First Ray, Divine Will, directed down through the layers of creation into our solar system through the many levels of your being. It is an energy of change, of allowing. When you invoke the First Ray, you step from that point of sameness onto the path of evolution and change. Divine Will is a characteristic of a higher consciousness, the drive and determination beyond the ego. It is a characteristic of the warrior, and you will find it helpful when great change has taken place. It comes to you through your soul, stepping down into your personality, into your atomic structure and helps bring greater awareness and vision to the larger picture.

Focus again on the particular stressor that you chose to work on today. The one stressor that you would like to lessen or eliminate altogether. Allow this energy of the First Ray to make you aware of the source of this stressor. Take this time to allow the answer to enter into your awareness. Silently ask what the source of the stressor is and allow the answer to come. Remember that you don't have to be concerned with moving beyond the stress right now. For now, we are just concerned with identifying the source of it.

(Pause one minute.)

In a minute we will begin our journey back. Use this remaining time to communicate with your guides and teachers or any other entities who might have joined you today. Ask them if they have anything else to share with you today. Thank them for their continued help and guidance. Thank them for being here with you today.

When you are ready to return, begin your journey back by taking a gentle, deep breath. Slowly exhale, and as you do, begin to feel your fingers and your toes and begin to gently move them. As you begin to wiggle your fingers and your toes, allow your consciousness to begin to fully return to your physical body. As you feel your consciousness fully returning to your physical body, become aware of your arms and your legs. And when you are ready, gently open your eyes and return to this place and this time.

Welcome back.

Take some time and write down the insights that you have received. If you don't have a clear understanding of the source of your stress, that is fine. Just be on the lookout for some indication or understanding to unfold that may share light on the cause. Not everyone gets an answer the first time. It may take more than one attempt, or it may simply come to you later.

_____

_____

_____

_____

Technique: STRESS REDUCTION

Personal Issues
Not enough time, money, or help.
Too tired to do anything more.
Unhappy, you never see things getting better.
Too much stress.

Desired Outcome
Reduce stress.
Be productive.
Get things done.
Feel full of energy.

Key Concepts
Stress is based on personal perception.
Our beliefs and our personal experiences create our perception of reality.
What stresses one person may not stress another.
Stress can be controlled.

Process
Identify the source of the stressors.
Create new personal beliefs.

Desired Outcomes
Reduce stress.
Have enough time, including time for yourself.

Undesired Outcomes
No answers were found. *(Suggestion: repeat the process. Stress is still powerful.)*

People who are lonely and depressed are three to ten times more likely to get sick and die prematurely than those who have a strong sense of love and community. I don't know any other single factor that affects our health—for better and for worse—to such a strong degree.

- DEAN ORNISH, MD,
"Dean Ornish Talks Lifestyle as Treatment at NYC's Integrative Healthcare Symposium." The Huffington Post Interview, www.huffingtonpost.com. February 12, 2012

CHAPTER 7

The Second Ray
Love and Wisdom
Divine Love

Have you ever felt unloved? I know I have. There are two potential sources for that feeling. The first and probably most common source is related to human love. And it can really be a source of loneliness. I firmly believe that most people have someone who loves them. The bigger problems can be related to self-worth and not feeling deserving of love. There are, of course, many other factors that contribute to a feeling of not receiving human love.

The second source of feeling lonely can come from feeling disconnected from Divine Love. Allow me to suggest that many individuals do not have a direct experience of Divine Love. For whatever reason, they have not felt connected directly to the Source or the Creator. One of the major concepts embodied in the metaphor of the Twelve Rays is that we have always been connected to Divine Love. Most of us have, however, created an illusion that we are disconnected.

What I would like to do here is take you through a technique that is based upon a feeling of separation from our higher selves and the Source.

Moving Beyond Loneliness

Loneliness is a feeling that I am sure most of us have experienced in our lifetimes. I would hazard a guess that most of us do not enjoy the feeling of loneliness. That is quite understandable. I believe that feeling lonely is normal. I believe it is part of the human experience and probably can't be avoided. It seems to me that the experience of loneliness is also part of our motivation to come here in the first place.

I believe that we come into our lifetimes with intention. I also believe that it is our choice to experience life here. We have a great deal of say prior to our arrival in what we experience during our lifetimes. Living in this dimension, on this planet, allows us to experience a sense of separation from all other forms of life. That is a very unique experience, feeling separate. If you believe in an eternal soul that resides in another dimension, like I do, then it is reasonable to assume that in that other dimensions, we are connected to all other souls in ways that are not that easy for us to comprehend here.

Some may say that separation here in this dimension is only an illusion, and I agree to a certain extent that it is only an illusion, but it certainly seems real enough. Loneliness is a result of that sense of separation that is so much a part of this physical environment.

I'm not sure anyone can escape the experience of loneliness, but I am very sure that everyone can move beyond it. Let's not get ahead of ourselves just yet. We need to think about loneliness in some greater detail.

Where does loneliness come from? What are the sources of loneliness? You can certainly be alone, by yourself, and not feel lonely. And I believe you can also be with a group of friends or acquaintances and feel lonely. The presence or absence of others then doesn't define loneliness, although it can certainly contribute to the feeling. It seems to me that loneliness comes from a feeling of being disconnected. The question is, "What do we feel disconnected from?"

Talking about My Generation

We live in a digital age where we are all connected to so much. I was born before this digital age, back when there was black and white television. Transistor radios were the latest rage because you could carry them in your hand. We were led to believe that happiness could be achieved by accumulating stuff.

So we sought out bigger and better. To show our status in the world, we needed a college diploma, a rewarding career, a bigger car, a house in the suburbs, and a beautiful family. We needed toys: sports cars, boats, vacation homes, and private golf courses. And as we accumulated all this stuff, we didn't feel any happier. We figured that we hadn't accumulated enough, and we needed more, until it occurred to us that our stuff wasn't making us happy.

Now we live in this digital age, and we are all connected. We've got the Internet and our phones, and our friends all have phones with Facebook, Instagram, Twitter, and so on. We can shop online for anything and have it delivered two days later or maybe even today if we are willing to pay the shipping. So with all this connectivity, are we any closer to being happy than we were back in the day when we were told that our stuff would make us happy? With all of this connectedness, are we still vulnerable to being lonely?

Humankind is being blasted with so much sensory information these days, more than we have ever experienced in our history. Being as connected as we are just increases the flow of information. Our brains are actually geared to ignoring information that we consider to be not pertinent. We primarily use our beliefs to categorize what is important and what can be ignored.

What if this connectedness is really just one big distraction? After all, that is what many of us in the baby boomer generation think the accumulation of all the stuff really was, one big distraction. So many of my generation get to their senior years and ask, "Is this all there is?" My answer is, "No, there is plenty more."

A Reality of Duality

When I use the term duality, I mean that there are opposites. There is night and day, black and white, hot and cold, male and female, etc. There is also connection and separation. From our souls' perspective, there is no experience of separation. There is only connection. However, from our perspective here in this dimension, there is a very strong sense of separation. One way to really understand something is to experience the opposite. How do you really understand hot, dark, night, or male unless you have experienced the opposing attribute?

I like to ask my clients if hot is good. Then I ask them if cold is good. Most quickly come to the realization that in order to answer the question, you need to have a context for it. Cold in the arctic is a totally different proposition from cold in the burning sun. And of course, the opposite is true. Hot in the tropics is not as desirable as hot in the arctic.

What happens when you have experienced both of the opposing attributes? What happens when you have experienced both hot and cold? You create a synthesis. You understand that what you are really talking about is the nature of temperature and that hot and cold are just extremes of temperature.

In order to fully understand connection, there needs to be an experience of separation. Once we have had both experiences, we understand that what we are really talking about is personal identity. Our perception of connection or separation directly influences our understanding of who we think we are. When our consciousness is in a different dimension and we feel connected, it is easy to identify ourselves as multidimensional entities. When our consciousness is here in this dimension, it is more difficult to think of ourselves as such beings.

One of the great rewards for having experienced life here on Earth is this experience of separation. Just imagine that you live somewhere with perfect weather. You would probably become so used to the weather that you would take it for granted. But throw in a couple of months of damp rain, sleet, snow, and ice, and that warm sunshine feels just like heaven. You get the picture. It is through contrast that we really appreciate what we have.

Dealing with Loneliness

It seems as though loneliness can hardly be avoided since it comes with the experience of separation. While that may be true, anyone can certainly move beyond loneliness. My opinion is that anytime you have experienced enough of something, be it a feeling, a situation, or a belief, you can say, "Thank you; I've had enough," and move on to the next thing. In this particular case, anytime you have experienced enough loneliness in your life, you can say, "Thank you; I've had enough," and you can create a connection. Perhaps the most important connection you can make is to yourself.

You can break through the illusion of separation and connect with a higher aspect of yourself. A good way to do that, to establish that connection, is through meditation. I have included an example of a meditation that is designed to help you move beyond that feeling of loneliness.

This is a practical application of the Second Ray, the Ray of Love and Wisdom. In this meditation you can invite in the Second Ray and feel yourself surrounded by Divine Love. And as you do that, you will remember your connection to your soul-level consciousness, a connection that you have always had. In fact, you have never been disconnected from your soul- level consciousness. This is where the illusion comes in. You have agreed to believe in the illusion of separation, but you can let go of that belief any time you choose.

Meditation: MOVING BEYOND LONELINESS

Here is a short mediation to help you move beyond the feeling of loneliness. Use this meditation to connect to your soul-level consciousness. Use it to help you remember the connection that has always been there.

Before you begin this exercise, I'd like to share with you some more information about the Second Ray. This comes directly from the Team: "We have allowed new energies into your dimension to brighten your world, to help you find that light, to reconnect with the love that you are, with the love that you always have been. Allow yourself to feel the love, to open your heart. Bless yourself, and as you do, your connection to your true self, your whole self, will open up. And as that connection opens, your love for your planet, for each blade of grass, for each insect and animal, and for each human, each human being, will open."

As we begin this meditation for the Second Ray, I'd like you to get comfortable in your chair if you are seated. You may prefer to sit on the floor. Choose whatever is most comfortable for you. If you have anything on your lap, please put it on the floor now. Now, gently relax your hands either in your lap or at your side. Have your feet resting comfortably beneath you, either on the floor or folded in some way. Take a relaxing, deep breath, breathing in fresh, clean air, and as you exhale, breathe out any stress or anxiety that you may be feeling. Continue to focus on your breath and maintain a gentle, rhythmic breathing pattern. Good.

Now focus your attention on the light of the Second Ray. Bring in the luminescent aqua-blue energy of the Second Ray and begin to wrap it around you. Start from your feet and wrap it around just like you were wrapping up an Egyptian mummy. Continue to wrap this energy around you until it forms an energetic cocoon all around you. And when you have completed wrapping yourself, take a moment and feel yourself surrounded by this beautiful energy of the Second Ray.

And now call forth the beautiful pink energy of Divine Love and move this energy around your heart. Envision your heart to be surrounded by this beautiful, pink energy of Divine Love. Take a moment and think about how you have protected your heart based upon your past experiences, your past hurts. Think about the defenses that you have established to protect your heart. Now feel this pink energy begin to penetrate those defenses and feel them begin to soften. We don't want to dismantle any of these defense mechanisms just now. We just want to feel them beginning to soften as this pink energy of love penetrates them.

Now connect to your heart, the physical organ in your chest. And ask it how it feels to be surrounded by this energy of love. Ask it if it is ready to open to a higher expression of love. Ask it if it is willing to work with you to allow this higher expression of love, this energy of the Second Ray, to be a part of your experience going forward.

(Wait one minute)

And as you contemplate opening your heart to this higher expression of love, know that before you can really offer love to anyone else you must first offer it to yourself. You must first be willing to forgive yourself and accept self-love. And once you have opened your heart to self-love, you clear the path to experience this higher love. But before you can truly love others, you must first love yourself.

(Wait one minute)

You are capable of opening fully to the love that is within your heart. Again, feel your heart surrounded by this beautiful, pink energy of the Second Ray, the energy of Divine Love. Feel it once again as it begins to soften all of those defenses that have been put in place to protect it. Know that you go at your own pace as you soften those defenses, never going any faster than you choose to. You are in complete control. Feel how good that feels.

And as you feel yourself surrounded by this beautiful, pink light, this energy of Divine Love, allow yourself to feel connected to the Source of this energy. Allow yourself to remember how it feels to be connected to this energy. And as you remember your connection to this energy, you realize that you have always been connected to this energy of Divine Love. You may have felt alone and isolated, perhaps feeling unsupported and on your own, but this has always been just an illusion. And this illusion had its purpose. It had its role to play. But now you feel connected once again to the Source of All Love and you see the illusion of separation as just that, an illusion. Allow yourself to remember who you really are and embrace the real you.

(Wait one minute)

In a minute we will begin to bring your awareness back to your physical body. Take this time to thank your heart for all the love that it holds for you. Thank it for all the ways that it has supported you so far in your journey. And thank it for its willingness to move forward with you as you open to this higher expression of love that the Second Ray reminds you of.

Offer your gratitude for remembering once again your connection to All That Is. Integrate this awareness with whom you know yourself to be in this dimension and allow yourself to gain a new perspective on life here in this physical dimension.

Now once again focus your awareness on your breathing. Take a gentle, deep breath, and as you do, begin to allow your consciousness to return to your physical body. Continue with your rhythmic breathing. Gently begin to wiggle your fingers and your toes, and as you do, once again feel the connection with your arms and your legs. Continue to allow your consciousness to return to your body, and when you are ready, gently open your eyes and return to this place and this time, fully relaxed and feeling calm and peaceful.

Welcome back.

Take some time and write down the insights that you have received. If the illusion of separation was the source of your loneliness, then you should have a better understanding of it now. If it wasn't, did you get clarity on the real source of your loneliness? If not, just be on the lookout for some indication or understanding to unfold that may share light on the cause. Not everyone gets an answer the first time. It may take more than one attempt, or it may simply come to you later.

_____

_____

_____

_____

Feel free to do this exercise anytime you wish to move beyond any feeling of loneliness. It will help you to strengthen your memory of your connection to your whole self. There is great purpose in experiencing loneliness. It helps us to understand the blessing of our connection to all of life. You have the power to move beyond loneliness when you are ready.

Technique: MOVING BEYOND LONELINESS

Personal Issues
You experience feeling lonely.
You experience bouts of sadness for no known reason.
You wonder what life is all about.

Desired Outcome
Find happiness.
Feel connected to a higher part of yourself.
Feel surrounded by Divine Love.
Allow yourself to feel loved.

Key Concepts
Feeling disconnected can cause loneliness.
Separation from others is part of this dimension's uniqueness.
You freely chose to come here.
Your life has intention, value, and meaning.

Process
Use the Second Ray to connect directly to Divine Love.

Desired Outcomes
You never feel such levels of loneliness again.
You can direct Divine Love into yourself and also others.

Undesired Outcomes
Still feeling lonely. *(Suggestion: repeat process. Loneliness is still powerful.)*
Unable to connect to the Second Ray. *(Suggestion: repeat process. Loneliness is still powerful.)*

You might say the First Ray energy says, "This is new; let's get it done," and the Second Ray energy says, "Do it with love and make sure the experience is true to yourself, your higher spirit." And the Third Ray says, "We must do this, and we must do this, and it must be done in this way, and that gets it done." It focuses on the practical, and you find individual entities with a lot of this energy tend to be stubborn and driven and focused on the outcome.

– THE TEAM

CHAPTER 8

The Third Ray
Active Intelligence
Manifesting Your Desires

In our earlier discussion, we talked about change and, in particular, resistance to change. There was a meditation designed to help you understand the source of any resistance to change. In the example that was given, I suggested that one possible source of resistance could be the fear of giving up control. If you took the time to do the meditation, I hope you found your individual source of resistance to the specific change that you were focused on.

If you didn't have time to do the previous meditation or you feel you weren't successful in identifying the real source of the resistance, then I suggest you do it either for the first time or again before you sit down to do the mediation that is part of this discussion.

If you have indeed connected with the source of your resistance, then think of a time in the past when you may have experienced an event that would have led to the belief that represents the resistance. One of the sources of our beliefs is our past experience.

Let's go back to our example. Just to refresh your memory, I used the example of wanting to use mass transportation to get to work instead of driving by yourself in your car. I suggested one of the possible sources of resistance could be a fear of loss of control. By the way, this is often the cause of the fear of flying. Continuing on with our hypothetical source of our resistance to change, imagine a time when the loss of control may have been an issue.

Let's hypothetically suppose that when you were younger, you and a friend wanted to go somewhere, say to a local ice cream store to get an ice cream cone. And let's further suppose it was too far to walk, and you only had one bicycle, and it was your friend's. Your bike had a flat tire. Your friend said, "Hop on my bike, and we can ride together." You began to ride, and your friend lost his or her balance, and you crashed and you were hurt. Maybe you bumped your head or skinned your knee. Because of that experience, you create a belief that is something like this: "It is dangerous for me when other people are in control."

Many of our beliefs about life come from real-world experiences. From that moment on, you have the belief that you need to be in control of what you are doing. That is actually a pretty good strategy and works well in many cases. But in other cases, it prevents you from doing certain things. Maybe you don't like to go to amusement parks. Could it be this same belief that makes it not fun to go on the rides? Generally speaking, any belief that you hold for one thing, you hold for similar things.

Thoughts Are Things

Over time, our thoughts become our beliefs. The beliefs can either come directly from an event, assuming it was significant enough, or they can come from our constant reliving of the event in our minds. Because our brains don't distinguish what we imagine in our minds from actual events, each time we think about the event in our minds, it is like actually reliving it. The more we think about it, the more likely it is to become a belief. Our thoughts and our beliefs create our reality. This is why it is very important to control our thinking.

Continuing on with our hypothetical scenario, you have discovered the source of the belief about the importance of being in control. How do you go about moving beyond that resistance and manifesting a change in your life? The simple answer is you create a plan, and in this plan, you are going to identify the steps needed, the proper sequence of taking action, and any resources you may need along the way to get you to your goal. Sounds pretty straightforward, doesn't it?

Coming up with the plan is not that hard. There is a handy tool that I would like to share with you that is well suited for creating plans for getting things done. It is called the Third Ray, the Ray of Active Intelligence. As a matter of fact, I refer to the Third Ray as the "Get 'er Done" Ray. The Third Ray is the last of the Rays in the group of Rays that I think of as our Divine Heritage. The First Ray, Divine Will, is where we get our ability to create thoughts and ideas. The Second Ray, Love and Wisdom, is our connection to Divine Love and the wisdom that is passed down with it. This Third Ray is the Ray of manifestation. We use this Ray to get the job done.

This works with any sort of task that we want to complete. If you want to build a greenhouse in your back yard, you could use this Ray to plan it out. If you want to plan a vacation, you could use this Ray to help you decide on your destination, what places to visit while you are there, and whom you want to bring along with you. And if you didn't have enough resources to pay for the vacation, you could even use the Third Ray to help you figure out how to get those resources.

The Law of Attraction

If you have heard of the Law of Attraction before, this may sound a lot like it to you. That is because the Law of Attraction is part of the Third Ray. You may have thought that the Law of Attraction was about attracting abundance into your life, and that is one aspect of it. I like to describe the Law of Attraction as also being able to attract the resources that you need to manifest your goals. Sometimes you require money to get something done. Other times you might need the help of someone else who has necessary talents and abilities, or you may simply need information that will help to get the job done. Whatever resources are needed, the Third Ray can help you attract them.

I'm not going to go into how to use the Third Ray here to attract resources to you. You can read about that process on my website, thetwelverays.com.

Just to be clear, you can also use the Third Ray to create a plan for manifesting a goal of yours even when you don't believe that there is resistance involved. Our purpose here is to use the Third Ray to create a plan to move beyond our resistance to change and manifest a goal we have selected.

Creating a Plan

Let's consider for a moment what constitutes a good plan for manifesting your desires. The first thing to consider is a time line. How big of a project are you considering and what is a reasonable time frame for its completion? If you are building a greenhouse in your backyard, a reasonable time frame might be a couple of weeks. If you have created a vision board and you have envisioned a new half million-dollar house to live in, that is probably going to take a little bit longer. If you are contemplating changing a belief, that could be anywhere from instantaneously to whenever based on your choices.

Next, consider the steps that are needed to achieve your goal. These may be unknown at the present time, and that's OK. You will more than likely receive insight into them during your meditation. If you are indeed not sure of the steps necessary to move beyond the resistance, then make sure you ask to receive that guidance during the meditation. And when you do get your answers to how to proceed, make sure you understand the sequence of the steps needed. You want to complete the steps in the proper order.

One remaining consideration is resources. Do you have everything that you need in order to get the job done? If you are not sure if you have everything, then simply ask if there is anything else that you require before you begin.

Take a moment and decide on what you want to work with now. It doesn't matter whether it is what is preventing you from making a change or what is causing you stress. Choose the one you want to create your plan for. Take a minute to write it down here.

_____

_____

_____

_____

Using what we have just gone over as an outline and having your goal clearly in your mind, you are now ready to begin the meditation below. As with the other meditations, I suggest that you read it through first in its entirety. Then either read it into a recording device that you have or go to my website and listen to the audio that I have prepared. You can find the audio file at thetwelverays.com. I hope you enjoy working with the energy of the Third Ray.

Meditation: THE THIRD RAY

As we begin this meditation for the Third Ray, the Ray of Active Intelligence, I suggest that you get comfortable in your chair or some other place where you can sit relaxed. Gently relax your hands either in your lap or at your side. Have your feet resting comfortably beneath you, either on the floor or folded in some way. You may start with your eyes either open or gently closed. Now take a relaxing, deep breath and, as you exhale, breathe out any stress or anxiety that you may be feeling. Continue to focus on your breath and maintain a gentle, rhythmic breathing pattern. Good.

Set your intention to use this Third Ray to create the plan to move beyond the resistance or the source of stress that you identified earlier. Focus your attention on the goal that you intend to manifest and use your imagination to see it already manifested. When you feel it already manifested, then connect with that feeling of it now being part of your reality. How does it feel to now have that as part of your experience in this dimension? And as you continue to hold that connection to your already manifested goal, allow the action steps required to move beyond that resistance or source of stress you identified to enter into your consciousness.

Let's begin using this golden-yellow energy, the energy of the Ray of Active Intelligence. See yourself in your sacred place, the place you go to feel your connection with your whole self. And as you feel that connection grow stronger, you remember your abilities as a cocreator of this reality.

You remember the way you manifest anything you choose in the higher dimensions. Now direct the energy of the Third Ray, this golden-yellow energy to flow through you. See it flowing around and through you anyway you choose.

Recall the issue that is creating your resistance to manifesting the change you wish to see in your life. If you are working with stress reduction, recall the source of stress that you identified earlier. Allow yourself to feel what it's like to have this change or stress reduction as part of your reality. Really feel it. Is it what you thought it would feel like, or is it perhaps more than even you had imagined? Allow that feeling of you having moved beyond your resistance or having reduced your stress level to be absolutely real for you. How does it feel?

(Wait one minute.)

Now while you feel the satisfaction of your completed goal, allow the steps that you must take to enter into your awareness. Allow the plan to move on to fully develop—or at least develop to the point that you know what to do next to accomplish your goal. You may not receive all the steps that are required right now. There may be choices you will have to make along the way, and depending on the choices you make, you may have a variety of possible steps to take. All those steps may not show up today, and that is fine. Just make sure you have enough to begin the process. Take a minute or two now to allow the plan to come into your awareness.

(Wait one minute.)

In a minute we will begin to bring your awareness back to your physical body. Before we do though, if there is any detail you feel you have not received, take a moment and ask how this will be communicated to you in the future and listen for a response.

(Wait ten seconds.)

When you have everything you need to create your plan to move beyond your resistance or to help you create your plan to lower your stress, send your appreciation to your whole self for supporting you in this journey, in this lifetime. Acknowledge the constant support that you receive that makes your experience here in this dimension possible. Remember that you are a constant projection of your whole self.

Now once again focus your awareness on your breathing. Take a gentle, deep breath, and as you do, begin to allow your consciousness to return to your physical body. Continue with your rhythmic breathing. Gently begin to wiggle your fingers and your toes, and as you do, once again feel the connection with your arms and your legs. Continue to allow your consciousness to return to your body, and when you are ready, gently open your eyes and return to this place and this time, fully relaxed and feeling calm and peaceful.

Welcome back.

Take some time and write down the insights that you have received. Remember as clearly as possible the recommendations that you were given for action. Also try to keep the proper sequence of the steps you have been given. Recall whether any additional resources were suggested, and if they were, how was it suggested that you would get them?

_____

_____

_____

_____

Once you have your action plan in place, you determine the timing of its execution. You decide when to start it. The plan may be simple and easy to perform, or it may be a little more complicated and take some time. Either way, my suggestion is to start sooner rather than later. You want to see benefits from the result as soon as possible.

Technique: CREATING A PLAN

Personal Issues
You have identified the source of the resistance to change and need to create a plan for moving on.
You have identified the source of the stress and need to create a plan for reducing stress.

Desired Outcome
You want to create a plan to move on.
You want to reduce stress.

Key Concepts
Thoughts are things.
Thoughts become beliefs when repeated over time.
Our beliefs shape our perception of reality.

Process
Connect to your inner guidance using the Third Ray.
Understand steps needed to take to move forward.

Desired Outcomes
A complete plan has been developed and can be acted upon.
All required resources have been identified and mobilized.

Undesired Outcomes
Plan is incomplete. *(Suggestion: repeat the process.)*
No connection was made to client's inner guidance. *(Suggestion: resistance is still strong. Redo First Ray step.)*

Until one is committed, there is
hesitancy, the chance to draw back.
Concerning all acts of initiative (and
creation), there is one elementary
truth, the ignorance of which kills
countless ideas and splendid plans:
that the moment one definitely
commits oneself, then Providence
moves too. All sorts of things occur to
help one that would never otherwise
have occurred. A whole stream of
events issues from the decision, raising
in one's favor all manner of unforeseen
incidents and meetings and material
assistance, which no man could have
dreamed would have come his way.
Whatever you can do, or dream you
can do, begin it. Boldness has genius,
power, and magic in it. Begin it now.

– W.H. MURRAY,
The Scottish Himalayan Expedition

CHAPTER 9

The Third Ray
Active Intelligence
Focusing Your Attention

(Also Known as the Law of Attraction)

I recently finished reading Dr. Joe Dispenza's book *Becoming Supernatural*. I highly recommend it, by the way. One of the points that he makes repeatedly is, "Where you place your attention is where you place your power." So when you focus your attention on something, an idea, a concept, a goal—well, actually anything—you are really focusing your personal power there.

This is actually how we create our reality. We all create things by focusing our personal power through our focused attention. When you jump into your car, you never get to your destination without first deciding where that destination is and second staying focused on how you get there. You have to focus on directions and street names and traffic. If you mix those details up, you are probably not going to arrive at your desired destination.

Humans are creators. We create our cities, cultures, countries, and civilizations. We also create our own realities through our personal experiences and our personal beliefs. These experiences and beliefs form a filter through which all of our sensory information is passed and decoded. How I interpret something might be very different from how you might interpret it. And that is a good thing. Conformity used to be a highly desirable personal trait. These days, not so much.

One of the Hermetic principles is the Law of Correspondence. It states that there is always a correspondence between the laws of phenomena of the various "planes" of being and life. "As above, so below; as below, so above." The reason this is relevant is if you believe that we are multidimensional beings, and when we create in the higher planes, we do it using our minds. We think about something, and it immediately becomes reality. That is because there is no time in these higher realms. I could speak more on that topic, but let's not get distracted.

As a matter of fact, the concept of time is one of the essential attributes of this dimension. It takes time to manifest our creations. And we need to hold our focus steady on our goals in order for them to manifest. Here is a part of a conversation I had with the Team about this concept of time and focusing our attention: "The whole process of the physical plane and the reason you as gods have created it is so the process of manifestation can be slowed down so that you can see its progression in linear, sequential time, whereas in the higher planes, it is instantaneous. When you have a desire, when you have a vision, the reality exists. In your dimension, it takes time and clarity to hold that vision. You must hold that vision for some time in order for it to manifest."

What I find most interesting about the above passage is the description of manifestation in the higher planes. We create simply by having a desire or a vision—a thought and whatever that is manifests instantaneously. In this physical plane with the characteristic of time, manifestation takes place over time, and we need to keep our attention focused on the desired goal.

This, in my opinion, is why some individuals have little success with the Law of Attraction. They forget to keep their attention focused on the goal. This ability of focusing our attention seems to be counter to the way our society is evolving in the twenty-first century. There is so much sensory stimulation—some say too much—that our attention is constantly being distracted this way or that way.

So is there a correct way to work with the Law of Attraction? One of the best processes that I have found is in the writing of Neville Goddard.

Neville Goddard

The story of Neville Goddard is pretty interesting. He was born on the island of Barbados in the early 1900s to British parents. He moved to New York City in the late 1920s to find fame and fortune on Broadway. Unfortunately, soon after his arrival, the economy collapsed with the crash of the stock market. With Broadway pretty much shut down, he found work doing other jobs.

This is when he met a turbaned, Ethiopian-born rabbi named Abdullah. They studied Hebrew, scripture, and the Kabbalah for five years together. It was Abdullah who gave Goddard the formula for attracting what you want in your life by believing it to be true.

When I first read about this technique in one of Wayne Dyer's books, I said to myself, "Wow. This is absolutely the Third Ray." I bought several of Goddard's books myself, and they are indeed a simple system for using the Third Ray. The technique that Goddard taught for manifesting anything that you desired has four steps to it.

First, there has to be a clear definition of the goal or the outcome. It can't be an expression of what you don't want to create. So something like, "I am sick and tired of not having enough money," is not a goal. Express the goal in a positive sense, and it needs to be clear and well defined. Even something like, "I want a well-paying new job," isn't very clear. What you mean by well-paying and what I mean by well-paying may be two entirely different things. A better goal would be, "I want a new job that pays $10,000 more a year than my present job."

Next, you have to create a concept of how you would know that you have achieved your goal. So using our example, you might say that receiving a written job offer at the new salary level would be a good indication that you have accomplished your goal. Great!

Now comes a very important part. How will you feel when you receive the sign that the goal has been accomplished? When you decide how you will feel, let's say happy and relieved, then induce a drowsy state where you can become attentive without effort. Now allow yourself to feel that way, the way you feel when you see the wish fulfilled. Imagine you have that job offer letter in your hand, and you are really feeling that feeling.

The final step while in this drowsy state is to stay focused on the goal and to believe that you have already achieved it. One way to do this is to create a gesture that acknowledges the wish fulfilled like, "Thank you, thank you, thank you." This is how you can manifest anything you choose to bring into your reality. Seems easy and straightforward, doesn't it?

The key aspect of manifesting that which you wish to create is focusing your attention on the outcome. When you become a master of focusing your attention, you will indeed reap the benefits.

Meditation: MANIFESTING YOUR DESIRES

The following meditation has been adapted from the writings of Neville Goddard. Use this meditation when you want to manifest something in your life. Before you begin, it is important to get very clear on what you want to manifest. If you say for example, "I want to be happy," that is too vague. Consider what would make you happy. Perhaps a loving, new relationship? Or a two-week vacation getaway? While you should be clear about what you want to manifest, at the same time you shouldn't be too precise. "I want a two-week vacation at Lake Tahoe between January 10 and January 24 of next year" is a little too specific. Set your intention for the goal—"I want to go skiing at a lovely resort this coming winter" is about the right level of detail. Take a minute and write down what you want to manifest.

_____

_____

_____

_____

Once you feel comfortable in what you want, then proceed with the following meditation. I suggest that you read it through first in its entirety. Then either read it into a recording device that you have or go to my website and listen to the audio that I have prepared. You can find the audio file at TheTwelveRays.com. I hope you enjoy working with the energy of the Third Ray.

As we begin this journey, I suggest that you get comfortable in your chair or some other place where you can sit relaxed. Gently relax your hands either in your lap or at your side. Have your feet resting comfortably beneath you, either on the floor or folded in some comfortable way. You may start with either your eyes open or gently closed.

Now, take a relaxing, deep breath and as you exhale, breathe out any stress or anxiety that you may be feeling. Continue to focus on your breath and maintain a gentle, rhythmic breathing pattern. Good.

Now imagine the golden-yellow light of the Third Ray and direct it to surround you. And as you feel yourself in this beautiful golden-yellow energy, allow the energy of the Third Ray to help facilitate the following technique of manifestation that has been adapted from the teachings of Neville Goddard.

In this guided journey today, we are going to focus on manifesting that which you desire to experience in your life. You already have all that you need. You have your imagination and your ability to focus your attention. Take another gentle breath and prepare to imagine your wishes fulfilled.

The first step in the process is referred to as desire. You must define that which you wish to manifest in your life. It helps to be as specific as possible. Choosing a goal like "I want to be rich," "I want to be happy," or "I want to be in love" is not very specific. What do rich, happy, or in love mean to you? How would you know that your wish has been fulfilled? Does rich mean a hundred dollars in your bank account? Does it mean a thousand, ten thousand, a hundred thousand, a million dollars in your bank account?

The same goes for happy. How would you know that you are happy? What would you compare it to? Be specific when choosing your goal and make it something that is meaningful for you. This is not about anyone other than yourself. What do you desire to manifest in your life? Go ahead now and choose the goal that you wish to manifest.

(Wait 30 seconds.)

After you have decided on a clear wish or goal, the next step is to construct an event that you believe you would encounter following the fulfillment of your desire, an event that implies the fulfillment of your desire. Decide on an event that will let you know that your wish has been fulfilled. It could be the letter with the new job offer. Think of a tangible sign that what you are manifesting has indeed become real. Decide on an appropriate event or sign now.

(Wait 30 seconds.)

The third step is to feel yourself in the proposed action. Imagine all the while that you are actually performing the action here and now. You must participate in the imaginary action, not merely stand back and look on, but feel that you are actually performing the action so that the imaginary sensation is real to you. It is important to always remember that the proposed action must be one that follows the fulfillment of your desire, one that implies fulfillment. Using our example of a new job, perhaps you are showing the letter to someone. Now feel how it feels to have the desired goal here and now.

(Wait 30 seconds.)

Do not visualize yourself at a distance in some future space and at a distance in some future time when you imagine the action after the fulfillment of your goal. Instead, make elsewhere here and the future now. See that event taking place here and now. The difference between feeling yourself in action here and now and visualizing yourself in action as though you were on a movie screen is the difference between success and failure.

And now the fourth step. The more you focus your attention on the fulfilled goal, the more likely you are to be successful. Focused attention will also aid in allowing the wish to be fulfilled sooner.

A most effective way to embody a desire or goal is to assume the feeling of the wish fulfilled and then repeat over and over again any short phrase that implies fulfillment of your desire, such as "thank you, thank you, thank you" as though addressing a higher power for having given you that which you desired. Allow that feeling to become so real to you that there is no question in your mind that you already have it.

It will be easy for you to remember to hold your attention on your desire, your wish that you now see as fulfilled, just as you now feel that you already possess it. Focused attention is the key to your success.

Now as we begin to return to your normal, waking state of consciousness, once again focus your awareness on your breathing. Take a gentle, deep breath, and as you do, begin to allow your consciousness to return to your physical body. Continue with your rhythmic breathing. Gently begin to wiggle your fingers and your toes, and as you do, once again feel the connection with your arms and your legs. Continue to allow your consciousness to return to your body, and when you are ready, gently open your eyes and return to this place and this time, fully relaxed and feeling calm and peaceful.

Welcome back.

Remember that you must keep your attention focused and do the daily work. I would also recommend that you set an intention at the beginning of the day that your goal is manifesting in the best possible time frame for you. Don't try to rush it.

Technique: LAW OF ATTRACTION

Personal Issues
You have trouble manifesting what you desire in life.
You have tried working with the Law of Attraction before but hasn't been very successful.
You experience low self-esteem.
You feel disempowered.

Desired Outcome
You learn how to focus your attention to manifest what you desire.
You learn how to work successfully with the Law of Attraction.
You feel your self-esteem increase.
You feel empowered.

Key Concepts
"Where you place your attention is where you place you power."
"As above, so below; as below, so above."
In the physical plane, manifestation takes place over time.
Manifestation is instantaneous in the higher dimensions.

Process
Follow Neville Goddard's four-step process to manifest what you desire using the Third Ray.

Desired Outcomes
Your desires are manifested.
Undesired Outcomes
Still not having success with the Law of Attraction. *(Review the steps.)*

CHAPTER 10

The Fun Part

Congratulations! You have experienced firsthand the Twelve Rays, in particular the first three Rays, in a most practical fashion. Hopefully, the message of the Rays resonates with you, and you see the potential that they offer.

I hope you really use your imaginations and find creative ways to integrate the Rays into your life. Please explore the music and the guided journeys that Richard Shulman and I have created. I believe it helps people connect even more deeply with the Rays. We constantly get positive feedback from individuals who are enjoying the music. I hope you will be able to integrate the music in some way in your individual work.

Each Ray is, in and of itself, broad and majestic. I feel that we are just scratching the surface of what these energies really represent. There are, of course, Twelve Rays, and each can be used in a variety of ways. We have intentionally focused in this workshop on the first three Rays. As more of us gain experience with the Rays and as more of us work with our imaginations to find creative new ways to apply them, I'm sure our understanding of them will grow greatly.

This workshop is the first of three workshops that are designed for individuals like you. The second individual workshop focuses on the Rays of Attributes, Rays Four through Seven, and the Eighth Ray, the Cleansing Ray. We use these Rays to help us have the human experiences that we planned before we ever incarnated in this lifetime. There is particular emphasis placed on the Seventh Ray and the Eighth Ray. The Seventh Ray is commonly referred to as the Violet Flame and is still used to dissolve the weightiness of past experience. But it is also referred to as the Gateway into Awareness. This new emphasis will be discussed in depth. There will also be new musical exercises to go along with these Rays.

The third workshop focuses on the Rays of Soul Integration. These are Rays

Nine through Twelve. This workshop will include exercises on connecting with your soul-level consciousness and the Body of Light. The Body of Light is the next step forward for humanity.

This third workshop will also feature exercises that will introduce the New Awareness. There is more on that to come.

Thank You

Thanks for taking an interest and investing your time and resources in the Twelve Rays. The Rays are new concepts for most, and it does take some time to really feel the scope and breadth of them. The more you work with them, the more natural they will feel to you.

This workshop has been focused on the practical applications that you can use every day. There is, however, much more to the Twelve Rays. There is a new cosmology, a new way of thinking and believing about this reality, that I believe really resonates with individuals whom I refer to as "want-to-believers." I use this term to describe individuals who have walked away from the religious traditions of childhood but have yet to find something new to believe in. I was one of them, and maybe you are too. The message of the Rays is to believe in yourself and to let your light shine.

NOTES

NOTES

What's Next?

Continue expanding your knowledge of
the Twelve Rays' practical applications
by attending the next workshop in the series.

Life Experiences Workshop
Rays Four through Seven

Learn techniques that use the Rays of Attributes, also called the Rays of
Experience. The Seventh Ray is of particular interest because you may
have heard of it already. The Seventh Ray is also called the Violet Flame
of St. Germain. You will learn to:

- Create harmony through conflict using the Fourth Ray.
- Balance yourself when you are overwhelmed by your emotions using
  the Fifth Ray.
- Focus your intentions, goals, and objectives with the Sixth Ray.
- Transmute the weightiness of past experience using the Seventh Ray.
- Cleanse and balance the emotional body using the Eight Ray.

Soul Integration Workshop
Rays Eight through Twelve

Work with the new Rays, which we refer to as the Rays of Soul
Integration, to establish contact with your soul-level consciousness and
begin to anchor the Body of Light into your current physical body here in
this dimension. You will learn to:

- Bring inner clarity through your third eye using the Eight Ray.
- Establish contact with your soul-level consciousness using the
  Ninth Ray.
- Establish contact with your Body of Light using the Ninth Ray.
- Begin to anchor your Body of Light into your physical structure.
- Connect with and direct Spiritual Microtrons.

Find more information about all the workshops at
thetwelverays.com/workshops

CPSIA information can be obtained
at www.ICGtesting.com
Printed in the USA
FSHW010613090619
58826FS